D1561101

# Explore
## the
# West

**Peter and Connie Roop**

**PICTURE CREDITS**

Cover © Jeff Vanuga/Corbis; title page © Bob Torrez/Getty Images; pages 2-3, 12 (bottom), 22, 31 (top right), 34-a, 35-c, 36 © Corbis; pages 4-5, 25 (top left), 35-b illustrations by Rose Zgodzinski; pages 6-7, 29 © Philip James Corwin/Corbis; pages 8, 30 (top left) © ML Sinibaldi/Corbis; pages 9 (top), 31 (center left), 34-b © Bob Krist/Corbis; page 9 (inset), 31 (center right) © David A. Northcott/Corbis; pages 10 (top), 25 (bottom left) © Underwood & Underwood/Corbis; page 10 (bottom) © Index Stock Imagery; pages 11, 18, 20, 30 (top right), 34-c, 35-f © The Granger Collection, New York; pages 12 (top), 35-e © Natalie Fobes/Corbis; pages 13, 35-d © Chris Close/Getty Images; pages 14, 30 (bottom left), 34-d © Kevin Horan/Getty Images; pages 15, 34-e © Mark Scott/Getty Images; pages 16-17 © John Kelly/Getty Images; pages 19, 31 (bottom left) © New-York Historical Society, New York/The Bridgeman Collection; page 21 © Bettmann/Corbis; page 23 © Bill Heinsohn/Getty Images; pages 25 (top right), 31 (bottom right) © David W. Hamilton/Getty Images; page 25 (bottom right) © Dwayne Newton/Photo Edit; page 26 © Kevin R. Morris/Corbis; page 27 © Ted Wood/Getty Images; page 28 (left) © Steve Terrill/Corbis; page 28 (right) © Jim Sugar/Getty Images; page 30 (bottom right) © John Lamb/Getty Images; page 31 (top left) © Panoramic Images/Getty Images; page 32 © Wolfgang Kaehler/Corbis; page 33 (left) The West by Elspeth Leacock, © 2002 National Geographic Society, photo © John Marshall/Stone/Getty Images; page 33 (center) The West: Its History and People by Gare Thompson, © 2003 National Geographic Society, photos © Hulton Archive/Getty Images; page 33 (right) The West Today, © 2004 National Geographic Society, photo © Charles O'Rear/Corbis; page 34-f © Douglas Peebles/Corbis; page 35-a © J. A. Kraulis/Masterfile.

Produced through the worldwide resources of the National Geographic Society, John M. Fahey, Jr., President and Chief Executive Officer; Gilbert M. Grosvenor, Chairman of the Board; Nina D. Hoffman, Executive Vice President and President, Books and Education Publishing Group.

**PREPARED BY NATIONAL GEOGRAPHIC SCHOOL PUBLISHING**

Ericka Markman, Senior Vice President and President, Children's Books and Education Publishing Group; Steve Mico, Senior Vice President, Editorial Director, Publisher; Francis Downey, Executive Editor; Richard Easby, Editorial Manager; Anne Stone, Lori Dibble Collins, Editors; Bea Jackson, Director of Layout and Design; Jim Hiscott, Design Manager; Cynthia Olson, Art Director; Margaret Sidlosky, Illustrations Director; Matt Wascavage, Manager of Publishing Services; Sean Philpotts, Production Manager; Ted Tucker, Production Specialist.

**MANUFACTURING AND QUALITY CONTROL**

Christopher A. Liedel, Chief Financial Officer; Phillip L. Schlosser, Director; Clifton M. Brown III, Manager

**CONSULTANT AND REVIEWER**

Mark H. Bockenhauer, Ph.D., Associate Professor of Geography, St. Norbert College, De Pere, Wisconsin

**BOOK DESIGN/PHOTO RESEARCH**

Steve Curtis Design, Inc.

◀ Seattle, Washington, is one of many big cities in the West.

# Contents

Copyright © 2006 National Geographic Society.
All Rights Reserved. Reproduction of the whole or any part of the
contents without written permission from the publisher is prohibited.
National Geographic, National Geographic School Publishing,
National Geographic Reading Expeditions, and the Yellow Border
are registered trademarks of the National Geographic Society.

Published by the National Geographic Society
1145 17th Street N.W.
Washington, D.C. 20036-4688

ISBN: 0-7922-5461-9

2010  2009  2008  2007  2006
1 2 3 4 5 6 7 8 9 10 11 12 13 14 15

Printed in Canada.

# Five Regions

The United States is a large country. It has 50 states. These states can be broken into five **regions,** or groups. The five regions are the Northeast, the Southeast, the Midwest, the Southwest, and the West.

A region is an area, such as a group of states, with something in common. Each region has its own history and kinds of land. Each region has its own **culture,** or way of life. In this book, you will read about the West region.

**region** – an area, such as a group of states, with something in common

**culture** – a way of life

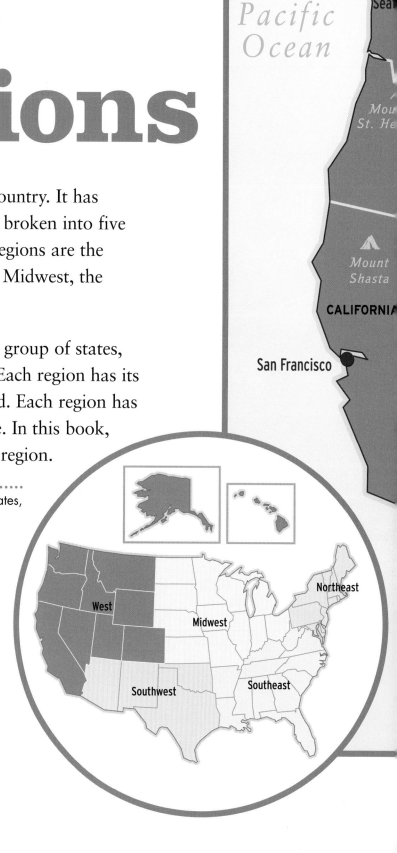

Pacific Ocean

Sea

Mou St. He

Mount Shasta

CALIFORNIA

San Francisco

West

Midwest

Northeast

Southwest

Southeast

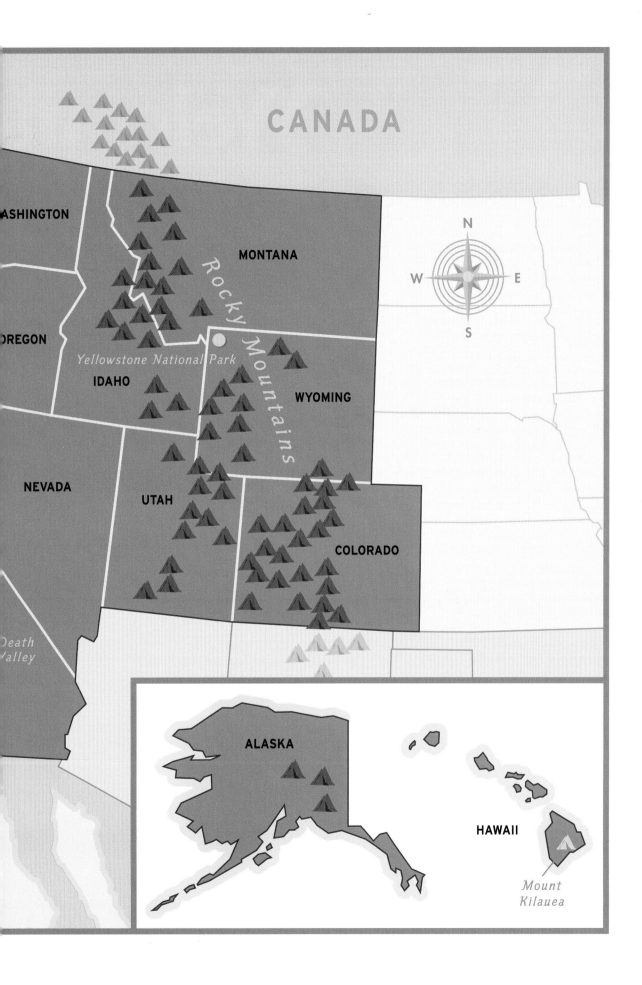

CANADA

ASHINGTON

MONTANA

*Rocky Mountains*

OREGON

Yellowstone National Park

IDAHO

WYOMING

NEVADA

UTAH

COLORADO

*Death Valley*

ALASKA

HAWAII

*Mount Kilauea*

N
W    E
S

# Welcome
# WE

**Big Idea**
The West is shaped by its geography, history, economy, and people.

**Set Purpose**
Read to learn about life in the West.

**— Questions You Will Explore —**

**What** brings people to the West?

**What** makes the West special?

# to the
# ST

The West is a large region. It has 11 states, including Alaska and Hawaii. The West has many different kinds of land. It has tall mountains topped with snow. It has hot deserts of sand. The West also has many rivers and lakes. Some states even touch the Pacific Ocean. There are wide open spaces in the West. There are big cities, too. Come explore the West!

▲ Some states in the West touch the Pacific Ocean.

▲ The Rocky Mountains are very tall and very long.

# The Rocky Mountains

The Rocky Mountains stretch from Canada to New Mexico. They are the longest chain of mountains in North America. The Rocky Mountains are 3,000 miles long. They are sometimes called the "Backbone of America." That is because they form a line, or "backbone," down the country. Some of the mountains are very tall. Snow stays on their tops all year long.

# Death Valley

Death Valley is a large **desert** in California. Death Valley is very hot. It is also very dry. Life in the desert is hard. But some living things have learned how to survive. Owls, snakes, geckos, and coyotes come out at night when it is cool. Cactus and other plants store water to use when the weather is dry.

▲ This gecko and other desert animals come out mostly at night.

..............................................
**desert** — a place that gets very little rain

▲ This man is panning for gold.

## The Gold Rush

Gold was discovered in California in 1848. At the time, few people lived there. Soon, thousands of people rushed to California. They wanted to find gold and get rich.

Most people did not end up finding gold. But many people liked the area, so they stayed. They started farms. They opened stores. In 1850, California became a state.

▲ This is a large nugget of gold.

# Crossing America

Traveling to the West was hard in the early 1800s. People followed trails over the land. They walked or rode in wagons. The trip lasted many months.

But that soon changed. In 1869, the first railroad to cross America was built. It was called the **transcontinental railroad.** Now people could reach the West in just a few days.

........................................................................

**transcontinental railroad** — a train line that crosses a large landmass such as America

▲ Trees are cut down to make paper, pencils, and other products.

# Timber

The West has many forests. For example, almost half of Oregon is covered by trees. Many people in the West are loggers. Their job is to cut down trees. Other people sell supplies to the loggers. The **timber** industry gives jobs to the West. Timber gives us products, too. Did you know that pencils and paper are made from trees? What else is made from trees?

**timber** – having to do with trees and wood

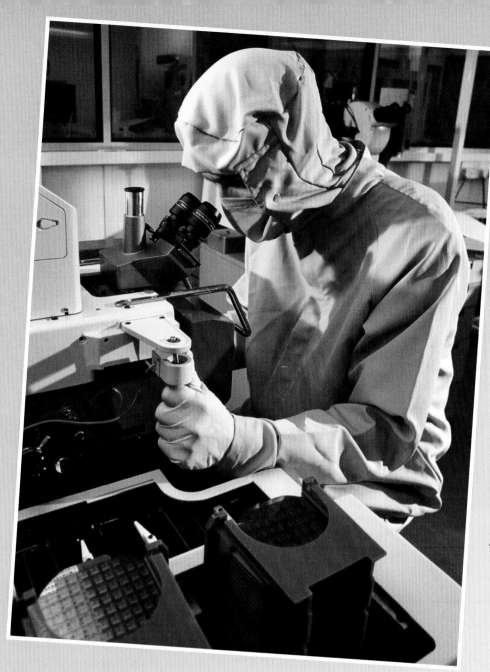

◀ **This person is making parts for computers.**

# Technology

Many people in the West have jobs in **technology.** For example, some people make computers. Some make **software,** or programs that run computers. One area of California is known for this kind of technology. It is called Silicon Valley. Products from Silicon Valley are sold around the world.

••••••••••••••••••••••••••••••••••••••••••••••••

**technology** – an industry that uses special knowledge to make things

**software** – the programs that make computers run

▲ A dogsled races in the Iditarod.

# A Race in Alaska

The states in the West have many things in common. But each state has a few special traditions. Alaska, far to the north, has the **Iditarod.** This is a race held every March. The race lasts 10 days. It celebrates the history of Alaska. Teams of dogs pull sleds across the snow and ice. The dog teams run 1,150 miles. The Iditarod is like no other race on Earth.

...........................................................

**Iditarod** – a famous sled dog race in Alaska

lei

◀ This girl is dancing at a luau. She is wearing a lei.

# A Feast in Hawaii

Hawaii is far to the west, in the Pacific Ocean. Hawaii has a tradition called a **luau.** A luau is a special feast. At a luau, people eat, dance, and listen to music. Each person is given a **lei.** This is a wreath of flowers, shells, or nuts. People wear leis around their necks. Leis are signs of friendship. The luau in Hawaii is just one of many traditions you can find in the West.

**Stop and Think!**

What is life like in the West?

..........................................................
**luau** – a special feast in Hawaii

**lei** – a necklace of flowers, shells, or nuts

15

Recap
Describe what life is like in the West.

Set Purpose
Learn about one famous city in the West, San Francisco.

# San Fr

San Francisco is one of the most famous cities in the world. It is found in northern California. It lies between the Pacific Ocean and the San Francisco Bay.

Two hundred years ago, few people lived in San Francisco. Today, many people live, work, and play here. Many more visit the city each year.

ancisco
# City by the Bay

# The First Settlers

Native Americans were the first people to live by the bay. They hunted on the land. They fished in the water. The gentle climate made this a good place to live.

People from Mexico began settling in the area in 1776. They built a fort and a church. They also built homes. Soon, they had large cattle ranches, too. They called the area where they lived Yerba Buena.

▲ Native Americans were the first people to live by the bay.

▲ Trade became an
important part of
life in the town.

# The City Grows

In the early 1800s, Americans started coming
to Yerba Buena. They wanted to trade with the
Mexicans and Native Americans. Soon, they
began to farm the area's rich soil. They built
homes and started stores. In 1847, people
gave the place a new name. They called it San
Francisco. San Francisco soon grew from a
small village into a big town.

# Gold!

Gold was discovered in California in 1848. The next year, thousands of people came west. They were called **forty-niners.** Can you guess why?

Many people hurried to pan for gold. But others set up shop in San Francisco. They made tools, tents, and clothes for the gold miners. They sold food to the miners. By 1851, around 30,000 people lived in San Francisco.

......................................................................

**forty-niner** – a person who went to California in 1849 to search for gold

▲ Forty-niners hurried to San Francisco to look for gold.

▲ San Francisco was in
ruins after the 1906
earthquake.

# Earthquake!

On April 18, 1906, an earthquake almost
destroyed the city. Buildings fell. Water and gas
pipes broke. Fires started and quickly spread.
Firemen tried to put out the fires. But the
earthquake had broken the water pipes.

Most people lost their homes that day. Three
thousand lost their lives. Still, the people of San
Francisco did not give up. They rebuilt their
beautiful city.

# Many Worlds

Today, people from around the world live in San Francisco. People come from Europe and Asia. They come from South America, too. They settle in different neighborhoods.

Each neighborhood has its own traditions. Each has its own foods and holidays. Each has a different language. Chinatown is one famous neighborhood. Many people come here to walk under the Dragon Gate.

**neighborhood** – a community of homes, stores, and people

▼ **The Dragon Gate is a famous landmark in Chinatown.**

▲ The Golden Gate Bridge

## Gateway to the Pacific

San Francisco is called the Gateway to the Pacific. It is easy to get to. Ships, trucks, and trains carry goods to and from the city.

Many tourists visit San Francisco each year. They look at the Golden Gate Bridge. They ride cable cars up the city's steep hills. They walk through its neighborhoods. They enjoy the city by the bay.

**Stop and Think!**

Why did San Francisco grow into such a big city?

BUSH

Recap
Explain why San Francisco grew into a large city.

Set Purpose
Read to learn more about the West.

CONNECT WHAT YOU HAVE LEARNED

# Explore the West

The West is a very large region. It has many different kinds of land. It is known for many wonderful things.

Here are some things that you learned about the West.

- The West has 11 states, including Alaska and Hawaii.
- The West has wide open spaces. It has many big cities, too.
- People moved to the West for many different reasons.
- Many communities in the West have their own special traditions.

**Check What You Have Learned**

**HOW** is the West shaped by its land, history, economy, and people?

▲ Some states in the West touch the Pacific Ocean.

▲ San Francisco is a famous city in the West.

▲ In 1849, many people came to California in search of gold.

▲ The West welcomes people from all over the world.

# Yellowstone Park

Yellowstone is the oldest national park in the world. It was created in 1872. Each year, millions of people come to Yellowstone. The park is full of natural wonders. Fountains of hot water called geysers blast into the sky. One geyser is called "Old Faithful." About every 80 minutes, hot water shoots up from Old Faithful. The water rises more than 100 feet into the air!

▶ **A geyser sends hot water high into the air.**

▶ **A smokejumper uses a parachute to land in the forest.**

# Forests on Fire!

Forests in the West catch fire every year.
Sometimes the fires are deep in the wilderness.
These fires are hard for firefighters to get to.
Who comes to fight these fires? Smokejumpers!
They put on parachutes and jump from airplanes
into the burning forests. They bring shovels and
other fire-fighting tools. The smokejumpers work
until the fires are out.

# Volcanoes

There are many volcanoes in the West. Some, like Mount Shasta, have not erupted for years. Others, like Kilauea, erupt all the time.

One famous volcano is Mount St. Helens in Washington. It last blew its top in 1980. The eruption knocked down forests. Rivers and lakes filled with mud. Fifty-seven people died. No one knows when the volcano will erupt again.

▼ Mount St. Helens erupted in 1980.

▲ Kilauea, in Hawaii, has been erupting since 1983.

# The Spanish Missions

The Spanish sent settlers to California in 1769. They were led by Father Junipero Serra. Father Serra was a Catholic priest. He and other priests built many mission churches in California. They wanted to teach their religion to Native Americans. Some large cities, such as San Diego and San Francisco, began as missions. Today, tourists visit the many old missions in California.

▼ This is the first mission started by Father Serra. It is in San Diego.

Many kinds of words are used in this book. Here you will learn about words that describe a person, place, or thing. You will also learn about words that are opposites.

## Adjectives

An adjective is a word that describes a person, place, or thing. An adjective often goes before the word it describes. Which words do the adjectives describe below?

The West has many **tall** mountains.

The first **transcontinental** railroad was completed in 1869.

A dogsled races across the **snowy** ground.

Tourists ride a cable car up the **steep** hills in San Francisco.

# Antonyms

An antonym is a word that means the opposite of another word. Look at the pairs of words below. What other antonyms do you know?

The West has many **open** spaces.

The West also has many **crowded** cities.

Death Valley is very **hot** and dry.

Animals come out at night when the desert is **cool.**

In the early 1800s, **few** people lived in San Francisco.

Today, **many** people live, work, and play in the city.

# Research and Write

## Write About the West

You read about the West. Now learn more about its history. Research the transcontinental railroad. Who built it? How long did it take to build? How did it change the West?

### Research
Collect books and reference materials, or go online.

### Read and Take Notes
As you read, take notes and draw pictures.

### Write
Now write an essay that tells about the railroad. Describe how the railroad was built. Explain how the train changed the West.

◀ This is a steam locomotive like the ones used on the transcontinental railroad.

# Read and Compare

## Read More About the West

Find and read other books about the West. As you read, think about these questions.

- What influences have shaped this region?
- What makes this region special?
- How is this region important to the rest of the country?

**Books to Read**

▲ Take a guided tour through the states of the West.

▲ Find out about the events and people that helped build the West.

▲ Learn more about the culture and contributions of the West.

# Glossary

KEY CONCEPT

**culture** (page 4)
A way of life
Chinatown has its own special culture.

**desert** (page 9)
A place that gets very little rain
Death Valley is a hot, dry desert.

**forty-niner** (page 20)
A person who went to California in 1849 to search for gold
The forty-niners dreamed of getting rich.

**Iditarod** (page 14)
A famous sled dog race in Alaska
The Iditarod is held in Alaska every year.

**lei** (page 15)
A necklace of flowers, shells, or nuts
A person wears a lei as a sign of friendship.

**luau** (page 15)
A special feast in Hawaii
A luau includes many traditional foods.

**neighborhood** (page 22)
A community of homes, stores, and people
San Francisco has many different neighborhoods.

**region** (page 4)
An area, such as a group of states, with something
in common
The West region has 11 states, including Alaska
and Hawaii.

**software** (page 13)
The programs that make computers run
Silicon Valley makes software to help computers work.

**technology** (page 13)
An industry that uses special knowledge to make things
Many people come to California for jobs in technology.

**timber** (page 12)
Having to do with trees and wood
The timber industry gives jobs and money to the West.

**transcontinental railroad** (page 11)
A train line that crosses a large landmass
such as America
The transcontinental railroad let people travel to
the West in days, not months.

# Index